YOUR KNOWLEDGE HAS VALUE

AF150385

- We will publish your bachelor's and
  master's thesis, essays and papers

- Your own eBook and book -
  sold worldwide in all relevant shops

- Earn money with each sale

Upload your text at www.GRIN.com
and publish for free

Vundavilli Gautham

The World Bank. An overview of history, structure and priorities

GRIN Publishing

Bibliographic information published by the German National Library:

The German National Library lists this publication in the National Bibliography; detailed bibliographic data are available on the Internet at http://dnb.dnb.de .

This book is copyright material and must not be copied, reproduced, transferred, distributed, leased, licensed or publicly performed or used in any way except as specifically permitted in writing by the publishers, as allowed under the terms and conditions under which it was purchased or as strictly permitted by applicable copyright law. Any unauthorized distribution or use of this text may be a direct infringement of the author s and publisher s rights and those responsible may be liable in law accordingly.

Imprint:

Copyright © 2014 GRIN Verlag GmbH
Print and binding: Books on Demand GmbH, Norderstedt Germany
ISBN: 978-3-656-89635-7

This book at GRIN:

http://www.grin.com/en/e-book/289318/the-world-bank-an-overview-of-history-structure-and-priorities

GRIN - Your knowledge has value

Since its foundation in 1998, GRIN has specialized in publishing academic texts by students, college teachers and other academics as e-book and printed book. The website www.grin.com is an ideal platform for presenting term papers, final papers, scientific essays, dissertations and specialist books.

Visit us on the internet:

http://www.grin.com/

http://www.facebook.com/grincom

http://www.twitter.com/grin_com

The World Bank

The World Bank is an international financial institution and is a member of the United Nations development group. The World Bank was originally established as a single institution in 1944 at Bretton Woods, USA. The governments of USA and UK played an active role in the establishment of the World Bank. The idea of the Bank was conceived by John Maynard Keynes and Harry White. During World War 2, the business classes of Europe were either supporting the Nazis or were forced to flee them. Socialists and communists had high credibility because they were seen as the leaders of the Nazi resistance. In order to prevent leftists from coming to power in Western Europe, it was crucial for the US and UK to get the business classes of Europe back into power. This required the establishment of strong institutions which would promote policies favouring development of private businesses. The fear of a post war economic depression also fostered the creation of the World Bank.

Accordingly, representatives of 44 nations met and decided to set up the International Bank for Reconstruction and Development (IBRD) and the International Monetary Fund (IMF). These are referred to as the Bretton woods sisters or twins. The IMF was established to smoothen global trade by reducing foreign exchange restrictions and help countries resolve their balance of payment crisis using the funds at the IMF's disposal .The IBRD focused on lending money to governments for long term economic development by building roads , railway lines, dams and other infrastructure . The IBRD was almost instantly referred to as the World Bank by the media and the name has remained ever since.

The IBRD began formal operations in 1946 .The bank's first loan was issued to France in 1947 for 250 million $. This is one of the largest loans ever made by the bank in real terms at 2.6 Billion $. As preconditions to this loan, France had to agree to prepare a balanced budget and give priority to repayment of this loan over other governments. The French government was also made to remove its members associated with the communist party before the loan was approved. Loans were also made to Luxembourg, Denmark and Sweden. The bank loaned close to 500 million $ (5.2 Billion $ in today's terms) to the post war reconstruction efforts .The world bank has established polices on the basis of the first few loans given by it . The loans granted are always at interest rates related to the borrowing costs of the bank, the funds go to only the intended project and never to finance trade deficits. The bank also receives priority in loan repayment over other governments.

In April 1948 President Harry Truman approved the Marshall plan which donated 13 billion $ (148 billion $ in today's terms)   to help with the recovery of European nations. Alternative sources of funds were now available for European Nations. Faced with this competition, the World Bank began to shift its focus towards developing countries. Over the course of time different institutions have been established under the World Bank umbrella which work in tandem, but have slightly different objectives and are separate legal entities. In 1960, the International Development Association (IDA) was established which granted highly concessional loans to the poorest countries. Nations which receive IDA loans have a ten year grace period after which they need to repay the loans. Repayment periods are usually about 40 years. These loans are referred to as soft loans. The IDA together with the IBRD is now referred to as the World Bank and these are a part of the 5 institute World Bank group which also includes the International Finance Corporation (IFC), International Centre for Settlement of Investment Disputes (ICSID) and Multi-Lateral Investment Guarantee Agency (MIGA). The IFC which was set up in 1956 provides loans to the private sector of a nation after being given a sovereign guarantee. The ICSID set up in 1966 provides facilities to help countries arbitrate investment disputes and has solved 283 cases so far. MIGA which was set up in 1988 promotes investments in emerging economies by offering guarantees to protect investors against losses from non-commercial risks.

The World Bank's priorities have evolved with time and this can be seen in its lending as well. In the first decade of its existence, it worked to assist in the reconstruction of Europe. In the 1950s and 1960s, investments in industry and infrastructure dominated its portfolio. The Bank used more direct methods to reduce poverty in the 1970s. Structural adjustments were focused on the 1980s. Sustainable development received importance in the 1990s and 2000s. Lending is currently based on a country partnership framework and the projects alignment to the eleven broad themes (rural development, human development, environmental management etc.) identified by the bank. The World Bank group has cumulative commitments of 1.067 trillion $ since its inception and 150 billion $ in outstanding loans to 35 countries. It currently makes yearly commitments in the range of 60 billion $. The bank has established concentration limits for each country. India has the highest single borrower exposure limit of 20 Billion $. A surcharge of 50 basis points is levied on loans above 17.5 Billion $. The bank has never written off any loans made to any country. The fact that the customers are also stakeholders in the Bank is an added incentive for loan repayment. The practice is to not reschedule interest or principal payments on loans. The bank has a policy of freezing loan approvals and disbursements if a country fails to pay obligations on time. The bank charges 1% over its costs on the loans lent through the IBRD to cover its administrative expenses which runs to the tune of 2.5 billion $ a year. The bank is a commercial organisation, which makes only a small profit given its scale of operations. It has made profits in the range of 600-1000 million $ in the last decade. The profit gained is put back into strengthening the banks operations.

The projects selected by the World Bank are funded by money raised from across the world's capitals markets. The World Bank raises 25-35 Billion $ annually through bonds. Each bond issue raises 2-4 Billion $ of capital with maturities ranging from 2 to 30 years. The coupon payments are either fixed, monthly or semi-annually. The World Bank also issues green bonds from which the money raised is spent exclusively on clean technologies and climate change related activities. The Bonds issued by the bank have been AAA rated for over 50 years. The AAA rating of the bonds allows it to borrow at a low rate of interest and can therefore provide cheaper funding for developing nations .The Banks bonds are among the safest instruments in the world. The bank is a very conservative organisation and has a maximum gearing ratio of 1:1. So far, it has only issued .59 $ for every $ of its statuary lending limit of 260 billion $. The bank can draw 41 billion $ from paid in capital and reserves and 219 billion $ from the callable capital of member nations. The callable capital is an amount which the member nations owe the bank, but are only required to give when asked by the Bank. There has never been a call on the member nation's callable capital.

All 188 member nations of the World Bank are represented by the Board of Governors. The Board of Governors are the ultimate policy makers at the bank. Each country appoints one Governor and one alternate governor to the Board of Directors. Aravind Mayaram is India's alternate governor to the World Bank .The Governor is usually the Finance minister or the head of the central bank of the respective countries. Each Governors voting power is equal to the financial contribution of the country he represents. They meet once a year at the Annual

Meetings of the Boards of Governors of the World Bank Group and the International Monetary Fund. These meetings are held twice in Washington and once in a member nation every three years. Close to ten thousand invitees attend these meetings and this serves as a forum for global cooperation and exchange of ideas. The five largest shareholders each appoint an executive director while the remaining nations elect their common executive directors. A total of 25 executive directors are selected who make up the Board of Directors. They work onsite at the bank and meet twice a week to oversee the banks business, policies, administrative budgets and country assistance strategies. The President of the bank is selected by the board of Directors for a five year renewable term and he is responsible for the overall working of the bank. The current President is Jim Yong Kim, a physician and anthropologist who was the President of Dartmouth College.

The World Banks position as the leading source of funds for development across the globe is currently being jeopardized because of two main factors – internal issues created by the bank itself such as the promotion of policy measures set as a prerequisite to lending which hurt client nations, criticism of corrupt lending practices at the Bank and the simultaneous rise of alternative sources of funding for developing nations which are more easily accessible and of greater quantum. The structural adjustment programs (SAP) of the bank have a less than one in two success rate. For those on the unfortunate side, the results are disastrous. Under a SAP, Tanzania was made to force its children to pay school fees. School enrolments subsequently nosedived across Tanzania. Throughout the 1980s Africa had an enrolment rate of 60%. The 90s saw an increase in the loans made to Africa (and SAP implementation) by the Bank along with a drop in student enrolment to 50%. The bank also makes nations subjected to SAP spend less on developing healthcare and basic amenities. This has resulted in a continuing spiral of poverty. Debt servicing levels continued to rise while living standards fell. Premature opening up of markets to global trade which is also advocated results in the death of local firms as they do not have the resources to compete with global giants and leads to economic shocks. Empirical studies have supported the conclusion that the world banks SAPs do not work and cited high level of recidivism and insignificant catalytic effects on other capital flows. It has also demanded abnormally high interest rates on some loans (Angola 22%, Brazil 44%, Congo 56%, Gambia 28%, Madagascar 60%), burdening nations which are already financially stressed .The banks President always having been an American reduces its credibility when it tries to promote policies on a global scale. The bank rather than being seen as a facilitator of global monetary flows has earned a reputation for being a controller of international monetary flows, often using its dominance to help or hurt nations at the behest of certain powerful countries. Surveys conducted among the banks staff show an organisation which lacks a sense of where it is heading. 60% of the staff think the bank places more importance on transactions than development. 58% do not understand the direction chosen by senior management and 68% do not think upper management acts as a unified team.

The bank is also seeing a reduction in its power due to the rise of other sources of funding which have grown to be much larger than the bank. The Banks' lending has also reduced in real terms in the last few years. Developing countries are increasingly financing themselves through regional development banks such as China Development Bank (CDB), Brazilian Development Bank (BNDES) and through remittances and FDI. The CDB had 886 billion$ in outstanding loans in 2011 as against only 136 billion from the IBRD. The BRICS development bank, now christened New Development Bank (NDB) reflects the dissatisfaction of the BRICS nations with the World Bank. The NDB has assigned each member nation one vote unlike the Word Bank and no nation has veto powers. The NDB established with an initial capital of 100 billion and a currency pool worth another 100 billion$ has an authorised annual lending limit of 34 billion $. The NDB is currently too small to act as a credible competitor to the World Bank but the situation could change with time and the addition of new members. Remittance flows to developing nations have been 13 times higher than World Bank lending and FDI 22 times World Bank lending. These are by far the largest sources of funds for most developing nations.

In effect, the World has currently entered a stage where the availability of capital itself is not an issue, but rather the favourability of the terms determine national borrowing. The World Bank would prolong its current existential crisis and risk irrelevance if it does not adapt quickly to the changed global economic environment. Changes in policy making and execution along with greater representation of the global community thereby taking into consideration all stakeholders would go a long way in helping the bank realise its true potential for positive global change .

References

http://www.iie.com/publications/papers/paper.cfm?ResearchID=403

http://www.globalexchange.org/resources/wbimf/stiglitz

https://openknowledge.worldbank.org/

http://treasury.worldbank.org/documents/IBRDInvestorPresentation.pdf

http://www.bicusa.org/wp-content/uploads/2014/07/Some-Evolving-Trends-at-the-World-Bank.pdf

http://www.globalissues.org/article/3/structural-adjustment-a-major-cause-of-poverty

http://www.brettonwoodsproject.org/2005/08/art-320869/

http://www.globalization101.org/why-is-the-world-bank-controversial/

The World Bank Archives

The World Bank Annual Report, 2014

The World Bank Group A to Z